HOW TO LOCATE AND SET-UP A BUSINESS NICHE THAT BRINGS PROFIT IN 1 HOUR OR LESS

Say Goodbye To Years Of Frustration And Hello To Rapid Online Success

Gerhart Banks

Table Of Contents

INTRODUCTION

*"One of the most common issues facing developing brands is **differentiation.**"*

You want to make an impression and draw in a group of devoted customers. However, with over *627,000* new businesses emerging each year, that is easier said than done.

Finding the correct audience is one of the simplest methods to stand out in the thousands of other firms that are similar to yours in the expanding marketplace. Instead of just attempting to please everyone, consider how you can close a current market gap. Learn how to identify a lucrative specialty.

To identify a lucrative niche, first choose a sector that interests you, then look for a subset of customers that aren't receiving the consideration and care they need from other, "broader" companies.

You can add something genuinely distinctive to your brand and create a tribe of satisfied customers if you can identify what your audience needs from your industry. Thus, how do you distinguish between lucrative niche markets in your sector and those that are too specialized for the general public interest?

That's what our investigation will reveal. So get ready to be inspired and motivated as we begin this investigation of achievement via the prism of niche understanding. The success stories included within these pages are not just accounts of monetary gain but also guides for individuals looking for a less-traveled route, one where dreams can become reality in as little as one hour thanks to the strength of a lucrative niche.

CHAPTER ONE

Identifying A lucrative Niche: The Need For Focused Branding

The idea of niche marketing is not new.

To locate something specific, all you have to do is start with a general notion and delve further.

For example, while the brewery sector is huge, there were very few craft beer establishments that targeted consumers tired of large corporate brands when Brewdog first started. The key to identifying a lucrative niche for your business is to look for a specialty that will allow you to become more than a generalist.

Establishing a distinct online presence for your business is essential to drawing in devoted, lifelong clients. Profitable niche markets are desirable for reasons other than simply providing a unique offering compared to well-known companies. These specialized products succeed because they have a thorough understanding of the demands of their target market.

Your user personas will become more accurate the more you can focus on your business offering. This implies that highly targeted sales and marketing campaigns that target a certain demographic can be developed. As your company expands, you'll eventually be able to enter new markets and draw in new clients who are connected to your original user base.

Why Time Matters In Niche Selection

Since markets are dynamic and changing quickly, time is a critical factor when choosing a specialty. Finding and occupying a profitable niche quickly is essential for several reasons:

Market dynamics: Demands, trends, and tastes of consumers shift quickly. The longer it takes to choose a niche, the higher the chance that the market may change and the specialty you've picked may become less important or saturated.

Competitive edge: One edge over the competition is time sensitivity. Entrepreneurs can establish themselves as leaders, foster brand loyalty, and seize market share before competitors arrive by being the first to recognize and serve a niche.

Adaptability and Innovation: Quick niche selection fosters an innovative and adaptable culture. Quick-thinking business owners are more likely to adapt quickly to new trends, developments in technology, and shifts in consumer preferences, which helps them maintain their products current and in line with consumer demands.

Agile Decision-Making: Successful entrepreneurship is characterized by the capacity to make decisions quickly. Agile decision-making is essential for overcoming obstacles, modifying plans, and seizing new chances in the battle to carve out a lucrative niche.

Decreased Risk of Saturation: As more companies realize the potential of popular and lucrative niches, the risk of saturation can quickly increase. By moving quickly, entrepreneurs can reduce the chance of entering an oversaturated market and secure a position for themselves before the competition heats up.

Opportunity Cost: Every second lost on thought is a minute wasted. The lost potential for growth, revenue, and market impact that results from delaying niche selection is known as the opportunity cost.

Time is essentially a strategic asset when choosing a specialty since it allows business owners to move quickly through the complex business landscape, seize new opportunities, and create a solid presence in their target market before the tide of opportunity turns.

Essential Resources For Quick Decision Making

Making judgments quickly and with knowledge is crucial while negotiating the complex landscape of business. Successful entrepreneurs have a core set of tools at their disposal that help them make decisions quickly. The following are important resources for anyone looking to act quickly and wisely in the hectic world of business:

Market Research Tools: Make quick work of gathering information on consumer behavior, industry trends, and competitive environments by utilizing cutting-edge market research tools. Real-time analytics from tools like Statista, Google Trends, and SEMrush help guide strategic decisions.

Data Analytics Platforms: Quickly evaluate and analyze big datasets by utilizing the capabilities of data analytics platforms. Entrepreneurs can track critical performance indicators, adjust tactics on the fly, and make data-driven decisions with the help of platforms like Google Analytics, Mixpanel, and Tableau.

Industry Publications and Studies: Keep up with publications and studies from the industry that translate intricate market data into useful insights. Investing time-saving in trade journals, industry blogs, and reports from reliable sources improves your comprehension of market dynamics.

Networking and Mentoring: Create a network of mentors and colleagues in the field who can exchange experiences and offer insightful counsel. Establishing connections with experienced individuals facilitates swift information transfer, allowing entrepreneurs to gain insights from the accomplishments and errors of others.

Technology-Based Communication Platforms: Make use of effective communication tools to promote cooperation between stakeholders and team members.

Real-time communication is made possible by platforms like Slack, Microsoft Teams, and Zoom, which guarantee that decision-makers are informed and connected.

Apply frameworks for making decisions, such as the Eisenhower matrix, SWOT analysis, and cost-benefit analysis. These tools simplify the decision-making process by providing organized methods for quickly assessing choices.

Financial Modeling Software: To project possible outcomes and evaluate the financial sustainability of choices, use financial modeling software. Financial modeling platforms, QuickBooks, and Excel are examples of tools that help with making well-informed decisions that support organizational objectives.

Platforms for Customer Feedback: Use SurveyMonkey, Google Forms, or social media surveys to quickly collect customer feedback. When it comes to making swift changes to products, services, or marketing initiatives, customer insights are crucial.

News and Trend Tracking Tools: Use services like Feedly, Flipboard, or Google News to stay up to date on industry developments and world happenings. Making decisions quickly is facilitated by being aware of outside influences, particularly while adjusting to shifting market conditions.

Agile Project Management Platforms: To enable quick and flexible project planning, use agile project management platforms such as Jira, Asana, or Trello. These tools improve responsiveness to changing business needs, efficiency, and teamwork.

Having a well-stocked supply of these crucial tools allows business owners to act quickly and decisively in the fast-paced world of business, providing them a competitive advantage in ever-changing markets.

The Top 10 Most Popular And Best-Selling Online Niche Profits

Building an online business and saying *"Build it and customers will come"* is a terrible strategy.

In the offline world, it is possible to establish a conventional brick-and-mortar business, such as a pizza restaurant, open it, and people will come in and spend money just because it is there. No marketing, advertising, or promotion is required.

Nothing could be further from the truth in the world of the internet. Nobody will ever locate a new website you launch if you don't market, advertise, or promote it.

1. Health and Loss of Weight

The list includes P90X, Weight Watchers, Atkins, South Beach, and Keto diets. People have been fixated on being in shape and losing weight for millennia. And they're constantly on the lookout for the newest diet craze, workout regimen, or miracle medication to make it happen.

Businesses have been there to support them with items that assist them in doing this, including diet plans, exercise regimens, weight loss plans, and supplements. You can never go wrong in this field as a marketer. Almost every group in every nation on Earth is interested in this.

2. Relationships and Dating

Whether someone uses online dating services or is just looking for love or is in a relationship but finding it difficult to rekindle the spark, there are several items available in the dating and relationships niche to assist. When it comes to this area, which is one of the most important but challenging aspects of life, people are constantly in need of guidance.

Promoting dating websites is one of the possible businesses here; numerous dating services pay marketers commissions for bringing them new sign-ups. Additionally, you may advertise **"pick up"** manuals, books on improving communication and relationships, and more.

3. Health

Although there is some overlap between the health and fitness sectors and the weight loss and fitness markets, health is distinct enough to deserve a spot in the top 10.

More than ever, people are taking responsibility for their own health these days. When it comes to their health and what they should do to stay healthy, people don't always believe the government or their doctor. Products in this area are widely available: gluten-free, herbal cures, vitamins, detoxification, healing arts, and a wide range of products. Anything that will encourage a long-term, disease-free lifestyle can help you live longer.

4. Self-Development

This is a massive web niche that is also known as self-help. Books, videos, online training, coaching, and courses abound. There is a self-improvement product out there for everyone looking to boost their confidence, overcome difficulties or hardship, establish and accomplish goals, enjoy career success, or develop their sense of self.

5. Pets

Pets are adored by people. In the United States alone, there are thought to be 180 million dogs and cats.1.Not to mention the numerous snakes, guinea pigs, parrots, and other exotic pets that people own and care for. And if you've just visited a pet store, you know that owners of pets will spend whatever it takes and purchase almost everything related to pets. gourmet dog food, animal toys, and nutritious treats Heck, I've even seen leashes for cats and dog strollers.

Furthermore, I do not doubt that many dogs eat better than I do! Perhaps a little naive, but whatever.

6. Use the Internet to Earn Money

You can impart your knowledge on how to generate money online with this method. You may design your coaching packages, ebooks, courses, and information goods. Additionally, as an affiliate, you can advertise any programs or courses that have been very beneficial from other well-known marketers. You might be involved in the upcoming major launch initiative.

7. Building Wealth via Investing

People want to make money, let's face it. And they are aware that one method to do that is through investing in stocks, bonds, options, futures, FX, and other financial instruments. They've seen the headlines, with all those extremely wealthy investors and hedge fund millionaires making big money. They would like to take part in the activity.

8. Individual Budgeting

In the personal finance segment, there is a dearth of necessities related to credit scores, debt relief, mortgage refinancing, personal loans, etc. Individuals require assistance with money management or obtaining funds necessary for significant expenses.

Perhaps they require assistance in securing a reduced interest rate or in paying off debt. Maybe they are filing for bankruptcy and need assistance. In extreme circumstances, individuals may have received the dreaded IRS notice stating they are in arrears on their taxes.

9. Devices and Electronics

Whether it's a tablet or smartphone, mp3 player, computer speakers, smart home appliances, thumb drives, phone cases, or earbuds, etc. People have an obsession with accessories and gadgets. Everyone is interested in the newest technology (new iPhone, anyone?). And there are several ways you might profit from that.

Selling the goods as an affiliate through an online retailer like Amazon would be the simplest. Alternatively, you might import goods by connecting with foreign manufacturers and wholesalers via websites like Alibaba.com or Aliexpress.com.

10. Cosmetic Procedures

eliminating wrinkles, looking more vibrant, and having tighter, smoother skin. Many people want to look more handsome and youthful. Thus, creams, formulations, and other such items that claim to get rid of or lessen aging indications are highly sought after.

Skincare products, anti-aging cosmetic procedures, and other related products are quite profitable. This could be one of the biggest markets on our list of the top 10 lucrative niches because baby boomers are becoming older and are looking for ways to slow down the aging process.

Gaining knowledge About selecting A Lucrative Specialty Allows You to:

Easier prospects for growth:

There is less competition for your target demographic the smaller it is. It won't take as much effort for you to establish your superiority over the others. Furthermore, you will be able to establish an affinity with your target audience more quickly because you will have a greater understanding of them.

Reduced out-of-pocket costs:

Generally speaking, niche marketing is far less expensive than larger advertising campaigns. You don't need to spend as much money testing strategies and marketing campaigns because your audience is more manageable and easier to target.

More devoted clients:

Building a devoted following of customers who adore your goods and services is the key to identifying a lucrative niche. These supporters are the backbone of your business, contributing to its expansion and success. You've invested more time and energy in getting to know your clients, therefore they will be more invested in your firm.

Simpler aiming:

You'll be able to get to know your clients like never before if you know how to choose a lucrative niche. This greatly simplifies the process of identifying the ideal client.

Mentality leadership:

Selecting a lucrative niche to dominate also makes it simpler for your business to establish a strong brand. You will stand out as an authority in your field because of your specific area of expertise

What To Look For When Selecting A Profitable Niche

Finding a lucrative niche is one of the first things a business owner must do if they want to succeed in the modern business world.

Neil Patel specializes in business growth and marketing. Suze Orman is a financial planner, while Tony Robbins is an expert in personal development. Whether you're an individual entrepreneur or a company as a whole, there are thousands of industries and sub-sectors to investigate.

Finding the market to which you can truly add value and potential is often more important in identifying the ideal niche than trying to operate in too many areas at once. *These are but a few of the procedures needed to identify a lucrative niche.*

☐ **Step 1: Conduct study**

The tasks required to manage a successful business are extensive homework. Assessing your interest in several industries and identifying the one that most appeals to you are the first steps in determining which market is best for your company.

Consider this questions:
–Which niches are you most frequently involved with? Which brands do you already purchase from, and which categories of their product line appeal to you?

–What are your greatest life passions? What piques your curiosity? What do you like to do for fun, and how much time do you spend on it?

–How would your ideal company be set up? Do you have any areas of expertise that you've always wanted to expand on?

–What abilities do you now possess? Do you possess any unique skills or past experiences that might be useful to you as you develop a successful business?

Finding a lucrative niche requires more than simply enthusiasm, but if you're enthusiastic about your business, it will be a lot simpler to turn an idea into a success. Even if you launch a firm in a market where there is a lot of room for growth, you may not initially be making much money. If you're doing something you love, it's simpler to struggle and live on a modest wage.

☐ Step 2: Determine which actual issues need to be addressed

Solutions are the foundation of the most successful companies. Put another way, business owners identify the kinds of challenges that their clients have daily and work to discover solutions. Examining the kinds of problems you have as a client in particular sectors is one of the simplest methods to identify a problem you can fix.

For example, perhaps you have a lactose intolerance but you adore pizza. How can you create a pizza that will allow those who could be similar to you to enjoy their meal without getting sick? *Among the methods you might use to locate issues are:*

–Talk to the audience you want to target: You most likely already know the industry you want to work in, even if you're not quite sure what things you want to sell. Engage in one-on-one discussions with locals to learn about their daily concerns.

–Look via websites and forums: You can find successful niche markets by researching websites like Quora and Reddit. People are constantly looking for answers to issues on these boards. You can discover the motivation you require to launch a new company.

–**Examine your intended audience:** Begin assembling a test group of individuals with whom you can communicate and obtain data. You may be able to join groups on Facebook, LinkedIn, and other social media platforms, for example. You can access concerns in your industry by launching polls and surveys here.

☐ Step 3: Evaluate yourself against the opposition

Examining existing offerings in a specific area is a simple method to identify a void that your new venture can bridge. If you were starting a business today, who would your closest rivals be, and what advantages they might have?

Finding out what you can do better than others isn't the only goal of competitor analysis when searching for a lucrative niche. Rather, you should concentrate on what sets your business apart from competitors.

If you work for a food firm, for example, your rivals may supply meals and snacks that are comparable to yours, but they might not cater to the needs of underserved populations in the community, such as those who are vegan or have gluten sensitivity. List all the topics you'd like to pursue and then see if you can delve any further. For example, consider whether you could sell eco-friendly clothing to consumers who care about protecting the environment, rather than merely choosing what you want to sell clothes.

CHAPTER TWO

Are you unsure about the characteristics of a lucrative niche?

Profitable Niche Market Examples

It's challenging to expand a successful firm in today's environment.

It gets even more difficult when you're attempting to establish your company's brand in an industry already crowded with rival companies. Narrowing down your target market at launch may result in a smaller initial customer base, but it will also increase your chances of success.

Are you unsure about the characteristics of a lucrative niche?

To get you going, consider these few instances.

- **1. Lefty's: The business on the left**

Were you aware that 10% of people on the planet are left-handed?

Despite this, finding left-handed versions of essential items like kitchenware, scissors, and other items at the typical store is infamously difficult. San Francisco-based Lefty's is a store that specializes in clothing for left-handed individuals.

Not only does Lefty's cater to a particular demographic, but the company does well in search engine optimization thanks to its decision to concentrate on a small but lucrative niche. With PPC, the business may bid on less expensive keywords and draw in a more niche clientele.

For the lefty in your life, there are even gift sets designed for lefties.

- **2. Natural Foods**

You most likely consider Whole Foods to be a major corporate brand these days. But like a lot of other prosperous companies, this one began as a specialty shop. When Whole Foods originally entered the food and beverage business, a certain segment of its clientele was drawn to the store because they were looking to eat healthier and buy premium produce and organic foods.

Naturally, organic food has gained a lot of general acceptance in recent years. Nonetheless, Whole Foods was able to lead the way because it saw the global need for improved well-being and health. Whole Foods saw the market demand poised to explode and seized the opportunity because it knew how to identify a lucrative niche.

They now have an app that allows users to get exclusive coupons, which contributes to the tribe's expansion. The Whole Foods website features a fantastic blog specifically catering to foodies, and the company also maintains a distinctive social media presence.

- **3. Lush**

One more instance of a lucrative niche that began with a straightforward concept for a small market. Unlike any other cosmetics company in the market today, Lush offers products that are natural, cruelty-free, and ethical in addition to being excellent, high-quality goods. The company constantly takes environmental responsibility and never conducts animal testing.

Lush was founded as a straightforward reaction to the dissatisfaction of those in the health and beauty industry who were purchasing goods that had been subjected to animal testing. The company developed a cult-like following over time as consumer demand for green products increased.

These days, Lush markets its products using a variety of strategies, such as clever influencer marketing and humorous copywriting. But the core of its success is in its devoted fan base, who never stop telling their friends and family about Lush's advantages. On their Instagram page, Lush writes, *"Here's to the #LushCommunity, where everyone is welcome, always."*

How To Determine The Profitability Of Your Niche

It's time to test your ideas if you've been doing your investigation and believe you may have discovered some profitable niche markets. Even though you may not have focused your approach in one area, you most likely have a few ideas that you think are solid.

Here's how to determine whether a specialty is a fleeting fad or genuinely lucrative.

- **1. Determine what is in demand.**

A prosperous niche must provide you with a product or service that you can market. Examining what is already selling in your chosen business is one of the finest ways to identify a lucrative niche. Checking out some of the best products in your market on websites like Amazon and others is a smart approach to accomplish this.

Make a list of the products that consistently seem to be doing well in your store, then consider what you could change to better suit a certain customer base. For example, may your company offer a variety of skin tones if you observe that customers consistently purchase a particular type of cosmetics to have better coverage? Could you modify the recipe to accommodate different types of skin? If there are many customers purchasing something like your main product, there's a strong probability your new venture will be successful as well.

- **2. Take a peek at what folks are looking for**

You can also determine whether a niche is successful by looking at what people are searching for, provided that there isn't anything too close to your product already available on the market. For example, Clickbank is a great resource to learn what people are looking for in your sector. Here, you can peruse the best goods and services available in your category.

The ideal product has few competitors and appears to be of some interest to the general population. You've found a potentially lucrative niche if you notice that a lot of individuals are looking for solutions to problems but are having trouble finding them online.

- **3. Confirm your concept on social media**

After determining the types of keywords that people are using when looking online, you can delve further into their queries to discover more about potentially lucrative niche markets. People regularly gather on social media to discuss items in particular industries and to address problems. For example, you can find groups on LinkedIn for business owners looking for useful accounting software, or groups on Facebook devoted to items for working mothers.

Examining specialized communities on Quora, Reddit, Facebook, LinkedIn, and other platforms will assist you in gathering more valuable insights regarding the features and benefits your new product must offer. To find out what you're missing, you can also post queries of your own on these social media platforms. For example, if you want to start a gluten-free cupcake bakery in your community, post a question on a local Facebook group to see if anyone knows where you can get anything comparable in the area. This will highlight the whereabouts of your rivals.

- **4. Choose your spot to stand out**

Even if you are successful in identifying a lucrative niche, someone else may have already crossed the finish line before you. Having said that, you will still need to determine what sets you apart from or makes you superior to your rivals.

For instance, what will set you apart from the competition if you're selling the previously described gluten-free cupcakes but someone else in your community is already offering something comparable? Is there a distinct voice you can use in your branding and on your website to captivate potential customers? Do you use eco-friendly procedures that will set you apart from the eco-conscious clients in your industry?

It won't last very long to focus on offering a "cheaper price" as your USP. It's always possible that your rival will cut their pricing to force you out of business.

- **5. Give your concept a try**

Testing your idea is the final stage in determining how to find a profitable niche after you've completed all of your research. Creating a landing page for your product's pre-sales is one of the greatest strategies to accomplish this. In addition, you can use forums, social media, and even paid advertising to increase traffic to that website.

A continual stream of Kickstarter campaigns is launched to test the viability of corporate executives' ideas. You can A/B test your approach even if you don't have many pre-sales to see whether you need to modify your messaging and begin acquiring clients for your future business. Just keep in mind that you must be prepared to make changes if you discover that customers do not require or want your new goods or services.

There are many lucrative niche industries available, but there are also many businesses that aren't going to be helpful.

Will Tour Firm Expand As A Result Of A Lucrative Niche?

Starting a profitable business in a cutthroat market is extremely difficult.

But all it takes to increase your chances of success is identifying a suitable customer base.

In actuality, businesses have a lot of options available to them, even in this crowded market. All you have to do is make sure you're paying attention to the requirements of your community's underserved clients.

You can identify a successful niche if you can locate a portion of your market that hasn't been penetrated by competitors or if you can figure out how to provide a new service to a current clientele.

If you identify your niche well, you can start developing a brand around it that appeals to a certain demographic of devoted and loyal clients. These customers will eventually turn into brand ambassadors, supporting your expansion into new markets and areas while you continue to grow and prosper.

CHAPTER THREE

Overview Of Niche Market

In actuality, most businesses achieve amazing things when they begin with a specific purpose. Your company becomes more distinctive the more specialized it is. Ultimately, even though there are countless branding and advertising firms available, very few specialize in creating visual assets, brand building, and company naming.

The first question an entrepreneur should ask themselves before launching a new business is, "What makes my idea special?" A truly sustainable and scalable firm is focused, and this necessitates a carefully thought-out niche marketing strategy.

So, What Exactly Is A Niche Marketing?

After reading this book, you will have a definition of niche marketing that you can utilize to set your business apart and spur growth.

We're going to examine how a focused strategy might eventually yield larger, more comprehensive outcomes by providing you with a means of forging closer bonds with every client.

To identify your specialization, are you prepared?

Niche marketing: What is it? Your definition of niche marketing

To comprehend the query, "What is niche marketing?" To begin with, you need to comprehend what a **"niche market"** is.

A subset of a larger target market is known as a niche market. For example, if your business sells gluten-free protein bars, fitness and exercise aficionados can be among your target market. But you're also specifically searching for folks who wish to stay away from gluten. Numerous instances of niche marketing set their target audience apart based on factors such as hobbies, income groups, gender, and price preferences.

What makes defining specialized marketing necessary, then? The short answer is that you are not able to please everyone. It's easy to believe that everyone can benefit from your product or service when you initially start a business. Everyone wants a wonderful television, a terrific audio experience, or an excellent brand-building agency, after all.
More distinctive traits, however, are probably going to draw in a certain market even while some components of your product or service

will appeal to a wide audience. A decent TV, for example, may be appreciated by all, but only a portion of the market will be prepared to pay more for the highest-end model, which carries a premium price tag.

With the help of a niche marketing plan, you can abandon the all-encompassing approach to business that makes it difficult for you to connect with customers. By using niche marketing, you focus your efforts and financial resources on the target audience that is most likely to value, support, and invest in your brand.

With every market and business becoming more crowded, niche marketing offers you an additional means of standing out from the competition. You may demonstrate to your clients exactly what you do and who you can assist them with by using your niche marketing description. This may result in you losing out on some consumers who aren't the right fit for your brand, but it also increases the number of leads you have who are willing to stick with your business.

The benefits of next-level niche marketing

Being able to respond to the inquiry, "What is niche marketing?" also entails knowing why this strategy is so beneficial for your business.

Crucially, specialized marketing comes in various tiers. Some of the best examples of niche marketing strategies, for instance, feature businesses that target a particular smaller demographic. For instance, FreshBooks positions itself as a service for "small businesses and freelancers," setting itself apart from other accounting software providers.

Some businesses employ segmentation to split up a wider audience into many niches that they then target with different marketing approaches. Either way, you go, your marketing effectiveness will increase with a more focused approach.

You start to establish your brand identification as an authority in your industry when you focus on a particular demographic. Customers will naturally seek out *"specialists"* to assist them with their most urgent issues, thus you're more likely to gain the confidence of your clientele. ***Furthermore, a targeted marketing approach will:***

- **Make you stand out from the competitors:**

With niche marketing, you have a clear focus and can take a break from the game. This makes it clearer where you stand in the market of your choice and lessens the competition for your intended audience.

- **Save your cash:**

Anticipate a higher return on investment with specialist marketing. After all, the likelihood is that you will spend less money if you're only attempting to target the customers who are most likely to purchase your goods and services.

- **Amplify brand allegiance**

You'll be able to establish a connection with your actual tribe through your niche marketing approach. These ardent supporters will be an essential part of your company and can even assist you in drawing in new clients with recommendations and testimonies.

CHAPTER FOUR

"Recall that niche marketing offers the advantage of not requiring you to be everywhere at once."

Successful Specialized Marketing Plan Creation Advice

After learning the definition of niche marketing, you're probably prepared to launch your campaign. As you've seen above, niche marketing can be a very effective tactic that helps you establish your brand's trust in a certain industry and gives your company emphasis.

The main obstacle is that, compared to the conventional spray-and-pray method of advertising, a niche marketing strategy is frequently more intricate. To effectively communicate with your customers, you must learn their language and use their preferred channels. This procedure may require some time and perhaps the assistance of a specialized marketing firm if your intended customer group is small.

1. Determine your areas of interest and strength.

Analyzing your USP is often the greatest strategy to choose a specialized market for your brand. Determining the type of client your services and solutions are most appropriate for can be aided by understanding what makes your business special. However, if you haven't yet thought of a USP or even a product or service for your business, start by assessing your interests and strengths.

In the end, it's always a good idea to base your business around your strengths. Consider the individuals you enjoy working with, the issues you want someone would resolve on your behalf, and the people who you find appealing. Selecting a specialty that resonates with you will benefit you in developing buyer profiles and creating product features.

2. Develop personas for your users

After determining your niche, you must develop user personas to inform your niche marketing plan. Recall that not every client in your fundamental niche is the same just because you've identified it. You may find that you need to construct various user personas to suit your consumer base as you gain more knowledge about your target demographic and the marketplace.

By approaching every promotional move you make from the viewpoint of your target audience, your personas will assist you. Don't forget to add as much information as you can in these documents, such as each customer's age, location, history, and interests.

3. Recognize your competitors and industry

Selecting a specialized marketing approach ought to reduce the number of rivals you face as you carve out a niche for yourself in your sector. Nonetheless, there's a strong possibility that there exist individuals who resemble you and can provide goods with numerous comparable attributes. List the rivals that most closely resemble your offering.

Your niche marketing agency may assist you in doing a competition study, which will enable you to develop marketing strategies that highlight your unique abilities to audiences. You can also be able to generate more ideas for differentiating your niche marketing efforts with the aid of your competitor's study.

4. Pick your marketing channels wisely

Recall that you must concentrate on speaking to your particular target demographic once you have defined niche marketing for your company. Simply selecting words and phrases that resonate with your target audience is insufficient. Additionally, you must ensure that the platforms where they spend the most of their time are where you are putting your messaging.

The good news is that you can target considerably more precisely using a lot of the social media and email marketing platforms available today. It is now feasible to purchase adverts that target individuals who precisely match certain demographics, interests, and past experiences.

"Recall that niche marketing offers the advantage of not requiring you to be everywhere at once."

5. Check, modify, and try again

Setting up your niche marketing plan and then forgetting about it is usually not a good idea, as is the case with most marketing efforts. More than general promotion, niche marketing necessitates close observation to ensure you're receiving the necessary attention. Additionally, you may confirm the accuracy of your initial user personas by monitoring the results of your marketing campaigns. Businesses may discover that their target market is subject to shift.

You may lower your chances of losing clients and squandering money on ineffective tactics by closely monitoring your data. Pay close attention to your KPIs and be prepared to make last-minute campaign adjustments.

Qualities Of An Excellent Campaign For Niche Marketing

You most likely have a fairly clear definition of niche marketing by now.

We must address one crucial point, though, to ensure that you fully comprehend the response to the question, "What is niche marketing?"

A niche can be something your audience has never completely explored before; it doesn't have to be a tiny piece of a larger dessert. Just take a look at how popular gluten-free cuisine grew once individuals realized that eliminating specific foods from their diets could improve their health. Or think about how everyone wanted to be a part of the progressive tech niche, which is how high-tech smartphones became the standard.

Superb niche marketing appeals to both your ideal customers and the audience members who are still unaware that they are part of your tribe. This ultimately indicates that there are three essential components to a successful niche marketing strategy definition:

- **First niche marketing feature: Storytelling**

Developing a niche marketing strategy for many firms involves figuring out how to market not just a product but also an identity or way of life. All buyers of niche goods can identify as particular "types" of individuals. If you share your distinctive story with your clients, they might conclude that your brand belongs in their own story as well.

One great example of a specialized marketing company that created a compelling campaign around an inspirational tale is Sole Bicycles. The Sole Bicycles website features a story section that offers an insight into the type of clients the firm hopes to attract and extends an invitation to join that enticing niche. What serious cyclist doesn't find it appealing when a bike business considers their products to be "art" or "epic"?

☐ **The second aspect of niche marketing: exclusivity**

Many businesses are apprehensive about "niching down" because they fear that doing so may remove some prospective leads from their target market. In actuality, though, niche marketing makes it possible to appeal to a larger demographic as well as a particular group of clients by using the psychological concept of *"exclusivity."*

Using niche marketing, you can differentiate yourself from the competition by focusing on the undervalued and underserved segments within your business. You'll find that your clientele is more devoted, thankful, and loyal as a result of doing this.

Consider the Firebox name, for example. Firebox promotes itself as a business that offers eccentric things that are "not for everyone." However, the company identifies a target market that entices people to join this creative, autonomous, and alternative tribe in its *"Not for Everyone"* vision statement.

- **Third niche marketing feature: Distinction**

Lastly, the cornerstone of any specialized marketing plan is a distinction. In today's increasingly crowded business world, you need to be brave if you want to stand out, even if innumerable factors can make or break your brand.

Consider Budweiser as an example. The alcoholic beverage firm introduced its unique marketing approach during the Super Bowl with the #NotBackingDown initiative. Budweiser positioned itself as a firm that was especially "not" for enthusiasts of craft beer. The corporation embraced the notion of being a larger, more concentrated enterprise, setting itself away from the burgeoning craft brewing movement. With the help of this definition, Budweiser was able to welcome consumers into a certain group of beer enthusiasts.

CHAPTER FIVE

The Top Three Instances Of Niche Marketing Strategies

There isn't a single set of guidelines that works for every business because the whole point of niche marketing is to establish a connection with a very particular audience. However, by examining past instances of successful niche marketing, we can gain some insight into what it takes to establish a presence in a more specialized market.

We've compiled a list of some of the greatest niche marketing examples we could uncover, along with the takeaways from each campaign, to help you get your niche marketing plan off to a great start:

1. Lefties: Be aware of the market

Let's begin with the most evident niche marketing golden guideline. Researching your target market shouldn't be neglected just because your appeal is limited to a particular demographic. You will need to put in significantly more effort to engage a specialized audience.

–**Lefty's:** The Left-Hand Store is a fantastic illustration of a niche marketing plan that considers the demands of its target market.

To assist the 10% of people worldwide who use their left hand more often than their right, the Lefty's brand was established. Their entire marketing approach is geared toward left-handed individuals, even down to their emblem, which features a symbol of a left-handed thumbs-up.

2. Powell's Books: Engage your audience by doing more than just advertising

For your niche marketing plan to be effective, it is not only necessary to comprehend your target demographic but also to ensure that you can communicate with them more deeply. An all-encompassing marketing strategy won't cut it. Rather, you must create an advertising plan that targets the clients who are most important to your company.

Take a look around Portland, Oregon's Powell's City of Books bookstore. In a world where eBooks and digital files are becoming more and more common, this little business wants to concentrate on selling actual books written by regional writers. The company conducts real, in-person events for those looking for more genuine experiences to assist in promoting their efforts, in addition to their internet advertising.

Powell's Books is adept at engaging its audience on social media by responding to their inquiries about literature and even sharing thought-provoking podcasts about well-known books. They also have no problem with the odd influencer marketing tactic:

3. Wistia: Pay attention to your clients

Ultimately, you need to do much more than just identify and comprehend your target demographic if you want to nail your niche marketing approach and make sure it continues to be effective for years to come.

The most successful instances of niche marketing originate from those who persistently pay attention to their target audience and address their requirements.

It's difficult to keep track of every mention of your brand on social media and other online forums. But the more you pay attention to your target market, the more probable it is that your brand will become known for speaking to that crucial subset of consumers you refer to as your tribe.

Compared to a corporation that invests in mass marketing, you have fewer clients to target, so you can spend more time listening to what they have to say. The insights you gain may also enable you to give your clients a more remarkable experience.

For example, the video hosting company Wistia increased the number of videos you could upload on your "free" account from three to fifty after listening to consumer feedback. Because of the tremendous social media response, Wistia saw an increase in user numbers from a pitiful 3,000 to 110,000. Even while free customers might not be paying for their service, Wistia is nevertheless building brand recognition and generating revenue from their free platform's adverts. Win-win situation.

Is It time To Consult A Specialty Marketing company?

You don't have to be everything to everyone to succeed in today's digital economy, as evidenced by the growing influence of niche marketing.

It appears that the brands that are most focused are the ones that do the best.

With niche marketing, you may reach a spoiled and overindulged audience without having to fight with other well-known businesses. You provide a real answer to an inadequately targeted space, as opposed to introducing a different flavor of the same product to a bunch of indifferent consumers.

You can find success that you couldn't achieve anywhere else by using a niche marketing strategy to identify the chances that exist within a hitherto unexplored market niche. The businesses with the most enviable reputations and the most devoted clientele are frequently the ones that prosper in the field of niche marketing. After all, you're helping those who have trouble finding
ng a solution in the current market—you're not just doing the same thing in a different method.
Of course, specialized campaigns require a lot of planning, concentration, and time, just

like any other marketing technique. It's important to get to know your audience, learn what they need from you, and provide value in a way that sets you apart from the competition.

CONCLUSION

There are many advantages to starting a business in a niche market, such as having a more focused and smaller customer base, being able to differentiate and specialize, having a better understanding of the needs and wants of your target market, having fewer competitors, having the potential for higher profit margins, being better able to build a strong brand image, and having more devoted customers.

In business, having a unique focus does not guarantee mediocrity or prevent your company from succeeding and expanding. In reality, if you construct your firm to master it first and then strategically grow with supplementary products or services, having a solitary concentration may be quite beneficial.

Finding the ideal niche for your company and improving your chances of success also depends on carrying out in-depth market research. You may differentiate your company from the competition and position it for success by concentrating on a particular and targeted customer base.